The Wing of the Swallow

By:

Ozodbek Yigitaliyev

© Taemeer Publications LLC
The Wing of the Swallow
by: Ozodbek Yigitaliyev
Edition: August '2023
Publisher:
Taemeer Publications LLC (Michigan, USA / Hyderabad, India)

ISBN 978-93-5872-124-9

© Taemeer Publications

Book	:	*The wing of the Swallow*
Author	:	Ozodbek Yigitaliyev
Publisher	:	Taemeer Publications
Year	:	'2023
Pages	:	28
Title Design	:	*Taemeer Web Design*

Foreword

Hello Dear Reader!

The book presented to you below is a compilation of the creative works of Ozodbek Yigitaliyev, one of the aspiring and diligent young people despite his age. This book is his first step into literature. This book of the owner is also a collection of his first paper drafts. This collection contains Ozodbek's memoirs dedicated to the memory of outstanding representatives of our literature, global and popular topics of the time, his feelings and experiences, as well as his first poetic works.

I have known him as a teacher since he first stepped into school. He is distinguished among his peers by his curiosity and ambition, his activeness in events, and his unique views on literature. At the root of his thirst for knowledge is the support of his environment and family members, especially his grandmother Muharramoy. the secret is too big. He doesn't waste his free time, probably because of his love for literature, he always writes papers; writes big short stories and articles. Until now, he is a participant of about 300 online and offline Olympiads, a prize winner of about 20 major competitions. He is also active as an active member of the All India Information System Council.

I have high hopes for Ozodbek. I wish him to continue to grow rich with the talent God has given him, without stopping his creativity, and to bravely overcome life's worries and difficult days to achieve great achievements. Not only I, but also his parents, relatives and friends hope that Ozodbek will become a person in the eyes of the people. - his brothers wish. I hope that he will justify our trust and achieve all his dreams and intentions and will not stop publishing new works for readers!

Mosayeva Adibakhan Abduhalimovna
Teacher of native language and literature at school 44 of Kuva district,
Head of the group "Young linguist"

Introduction to poems

Hello my head
I say hello to you.
Let me introduce myself
Then I'll tell you what I want.
I am my friend's confidant
I am a follower of Beruni
The Khorezmites are descended
I am a descendant of Alishers.
The place where I was born
It is rich in knowledge
The branch from which my people hang
His name is KORASHOKH.
Definitely in the future
I will be a psychologist.
Teacher justified your trust
I always go forward.
I am good to good people
I am against the bad guys.
My motto in life
I'm not tired of searching.
Even if there is evil
I will not go to him

Today we will introduce you to the classification of Abdulla Qadiri's story "Uloqda":
The story "Uloqda" is one of the first examples of modern Uzbek literature. The story was written in 1915 and published as a separate booklet in 1916 in Tashkent. In the story "Capricorn", the writer joyfully describes death side by side, encourages a person to always act wisely, and puts forward the idea of living in pursuit of enlightenment, spiritual growth and cultural life, without wasting life on useless things. Although this story was written in 1916, it was first published in Sharq Chechagi magazine in 1921. Despite the fact that it has been a century since the work was written, the events described in it attract the attention of readers with their originality, stylistic fluency, simplicity and expressiveness of the language. The story has been translated into many languages of the world.

Today's article will be devoted to the life and work of the great Russian writer Pushkin.
Alexander Sergeyevich Pushkin is a great Russian poet, the founder of Russian literature, the author of a number of poems, epic and lyrical epics, novellas.
Pushkin was born on June 6, 1799 in Moscow. By studying at the lyceum in Tsarskoye Selo, Pushkin entered the world of poetry. In 1820, he wrote the epic "Ruslan and Lyudmila". In 1822, he wrote the work "Prisoner of the Caucasus", as well as such works as "Boghchasaroy Fountain" (1822), "Gypsy" (1823-1824). "Boris Godunov" (1824-25) is a great example of Russian poetry.
After 1826, during the reign of Nicholas I, Pushkin wrote two long historical epics: "Poltava" (1828), "The Copper Horseman" (1833), "The Captain's Daughter" (1836).
Pushkin died on February 10, 1837 in St. Petersburg during a duel with Dantes.
I will end our conversation with the poet's poem "You and You".
You and you
The air is wrong for you
The girl suddenly said Sen.

This charming word burns in my heart,
A dream arose in my thoughts.

I'm so excited, I'm speechless.
I am completely under the spell.
I say on the surface: how good you are,
And in the heart: I love you.

Our article in Gal is about school.
School is a sacred place where human perfection is formed. School is the holy place that brought big dreams, lofty goals and aspirations to my little heart for the first time. School is the place where I first learned to write with a pencil in my hands and where I found my kind teacher.

Over the next two years, fundamental positive changes and comprehensive reforms are being implemented in the education system of our country. Many decrees and decisions adopted in our country are an important basis for setting up the training and education system of highly qualified personnel for the industry in line with world standards.

11-year education was introduced in general education schools in order to provide thorough and excellent education to young people, to bring education to a new level in terms of quality and content. This is the main factor in the correct organization of free time of young people, ensuring that they are constantly under the eyes of their parents and teachers, acquiring knowledge thoroughly and without distraction.

The decision of the President of August 14, 2018 "On the measures to bring up the youth spiritually, morally and physically, and raise the quality of the education system to a new level" creates wide opportunities in bringing it to a new level. Gold and silver medals were awarded to graduates of comprehensive schools, including specialized schools, schools of art and culture, boarding schools of Olympic reserves, and academic lyceums for their excellent knowledge, exemplary behavior and activity in public affairs.

All this is an opportunity for us young people.

In particular, great changes are taking place in the 44th general secondary school in Kuva district. Under the leadership of the school director, Jamoldin Mominov, free workshops, computer classes to improve the computer literacy of young people, and work to guide young students to the profession are being carried out. This school is the most advanced in the district It is considered one of the leading schools, and even some of its students are members of many international organizations and winners of many achievements.

We will conclude our article on this topic with the hope that the number of such schools will increase.

Today we will talk with you about the focus on youth.
I would like to start with the words of the President of the Republic of Uzbekistan Shavkat Miromonovich Mirziyoyev:
As a well-read and educated generation, you know very well that our country was one of the cradles of world civilization in the past. You are a descendant of Khorezmids, Farghanis, Beruni and Ibn Sina, Ulugbek, Navai and Babur, Bukhari and Termizi. The invaluable knowledge and discoveries created by our great compatriots are still serving the entire humanity today.
Shavkat Mirziyoyev

It is known that Uzbekistan is a country of young people. We are all witnesses that the policy of our country is aimed at supporting young people in every way. Since I have been working in the field of education for many years, I am very happy to see the conditions and opportunities created today.

Secondly, as a lawyer, the reason why I am writing this article in an upbeat mood is that the rights of young people are guaranteed in each of the implemented reforms. For example, the Law of the Republic of Uzbekistan "On the Basics of State Policy Regarding Youth" covers the issues of legal and social protection of young people, supporting their talents, while the Law "On Guarantees of Children's Rights" covers the powers of authorities and management bodies in this regard and other social issues related to the field. relations are regulated by law. Transferring students from foreign educational institutions to our own higher education institutions, testing procedures, testing knowledge in 5 HEIs at the same time are a vivid example of this.

I will take this opportunity to conclude my article by wishing all young people good luck, happiness, and not getting tired in the pursuit of knowledge.

Our article in Gal will talk with you about the reflection of patriotic ideas in the folk songs of the Uzbek people.
Uzbekistan is an ethnographic country. In other words, the land of Bakhshis. In addition, Uzbek folk epics tell about the distant past of our ancestors. The hopes and dreams of our people are embodied in them. Human qualities such as bravery, courage, patriotism, loyalty to the motherland are glorified in our epics. That is why it is an eternal legacy. The examples of Bakhshchik art not only bring pleasure to the listeners, but also plant the seeds of goodness in the hearts and spread the light of enlightenment. After listening to "Alpomish", "Gorogli", "Kuntugmish", you think that scholars, poets and scholars have not matured?!
That's why the president came up with a good initiative. Let's preserve this immortal heritage of ours so that the whole world can benefit from it, he said. In this way, the International Festival of the Art of Giving was founded, and this prestigious event was held every two years in the city of Termiz.
"Bakhshilar is not only an echo of the past, but also a resounding voice of today," said the head of our state at that time. Really, can evil come from a person who grew up learning from the way of life and bravery of our ancestors?!

Let's take a single Uzbek heroic epic - "Alpomish". There is so much wisdom and history in it. There is also a lot of interesting information about farming, animal husbandry, handicrafts, folk games.
The transition process of our ancestors from clan system to state system is also clearly reflected. In the example of the conflict between the Boybori brothers and the Boysaris! This is shown

in the case of the elder demanding taxes from his younger brother for the country's treasury.

"Alpomish" has another priceless value. Hakimbek's scene of bringing Barchin from the land of Kalmyks is expressed very impressively in the epic. Strange adventures, encounters with scumbags, bravery of the main character... On the basis of these, the idea of patriotism and fighting for the interests of the country comes to the fore. This gives the work the status of a national epic. The conclusion is instructive: love for the country is above personal interests!

The scene in the epic about saving his countrymen from the tyranny of the Kalmyks and returning them to the homeland also serves to strengthen the feelings of honor and patriotism in a person.

So, examples of folk art are priceless masterpieces embodying rich life experiences.

As a conclusion to the above thoughts, it can be said that we should preserve such cultural assets and pass them on to the next generation.

Goodness

Let's go for good
Let's stay away from evil.
My friends for the world
Let's do good deeds.

What would be left of us?
Wealth, the world or the state?
No, don't be mistaken, my friend
None of them will last forever.

I am my mother

I stroked my hair without sleeping at night
He asked Allah for good luck for me.
He counted the hours waiting for my ways

I'm the only one who depends on my happiness.

Al Khorezmi

Our grandfather Al Khorezmi
Great people.
Leading to good
They are always moving forward.
He created mathematics.
He revealed his secrets
Surprised the world
He spread the light of science.

Polite children

Autumn has come or autumn has come.
It came from thinking.
Apples, grapes, quinces
Pick it up guys.
And then I will give
Increased productivity
- No, no, said the children
Let him order
Your autumn harvest
We don't need it.
We have come to you
Give me a bag, grandpa.
- It's okay, my children
Happy dewy tulips

Seasons

Apples are ripe, quinces are falling
Autumn has arrived.
Farmers are busy
And we are running.
Ripe grapes shake
The sun is shining.
People enjoy it
Autumn is coming.

It rained and the sun came out.
The days are getting warmer
Trees are leafy
Peasants strike.
And this dear ones
They say spring has come.
It snowed little by little
There was a torrential downpour.
We played well
After we did it, it's fine

Shoahmad to my grandfather

You are a very kind person
You are a great person who works hard.
You are a beloved person who raised an orphan.
You are a dear person who will never be named.
Nina's father, Taras' mother
Sersenboy's father, Olop's mother.
There are four children, four kinds, and four horses
The greatest generation known as Shoahmad

Mother

Don't judge the mother
Mother is priceless.
Indeed, my friends, no one can determine the value of a mother. No breed in the world can be as kind and dear as a mother. They are honorable breeds that are ready to give their lives for our children.
Mother. With the sound of this song, our hearts are filled with pleasant expression and freshness. This is the love given to us by our mother, dear ones.
If we rely on statistical data, the more love a person receives, the more positive energy he emits. No one can give us this love more than our mother.

Another information: good qualities are passed on to us from our mother even when we are still in the mother's womb.
If any part of us hurts, if any part of our body hurts, then the heart of our mothers hurts. Because we are a part of the mother's heart.
There is no breed in the world
Kind like you
It's up to you
I am very nice.
An angel is without example
My flower
Be happy, my mother, stay healthy.

Congratulations to my mother

Mom! I love you so much. For me, you are the most precious treasure in this world.
I would like to conclude my thoughts with a poem about that famous mother:
I wouldn't trade the world for anything, every word is better than a thousand and one prayers
If the river is moistened with a drop of tears, I will do it
If you collect and pour all the poets, their poems on the top of a high mountain
What happened to 10,000 maduns for one piece of worthless Sooch
It is not shirk, forgive me, I am only circumambulating my mother
I prefer the water I drink from my head to a hundred thousand zam zam
If I know that my mother is alive, I am actually born of her love
Nurdayin pok oppppoq kabaku mother, and I am looking for a white kaba

The truth is, the world will be on fire if I miss my mother and cry
To me, poets are worth a dime, if your mother doesn't receive prayers.

Sayyid Abdulaziz Yusupov

The poet Abdulla Oripov

Abdulla Oripov is an Uzbek poet and public figure. Abdulla Oripov's work reveals one of the bright pages of modern Uzbek literature. His poems analyze the deep spiritual world of man and the history of the nation. In 1998, Abdulla Oripov was awarded the title of "Hero of Uzbekistan".

Abdulla Oripov was born in 1941 in the village of Nekuz, Kasonsoy district, Kashkadarya region. His father Orifboy Ubaidulla's son was a representative of the local collective farm. There were eight children in the family - four boys, four girls, Abdulla Oripov was the youngest. After graduating from high school in 1958 with a gold medal, Abdulla Oripov continued his studies at the Department of Journalism of the Faculty of Uzbek Philology of the State University of Uzbekistan.

In 1963, he graduated from the university with excellent grades and worked as an editor in the "Yosh Gvardiyachi" editorial office; (1967-1974) editor and chief editor of the literature and art editorial office named after Gafur Ghulam; (1974-1976) Head of the department in the magazine "Eastern Star". From 1972 to 1982, Abdulla Oripov worked as a literary consultant at the Writers' Union of Uzbekistan; (1982-1983) secretary of the Tashkent region branch of the Union of Writers; (1983-1985) editor-in-chief of "Gulkhan" magazine; Secretary from 1985, Chairman of Writers' Union of Uzbekistan from 1996 to 2009. In 1988, he was appointed the chairman of the Copyright Protection Committee of Uzbekistan.

Abdulla Oripov was the first and second convening deputy and senator of the Oliy Majlis (January 25, 2005).

In 1998, Abdulla Oripov was awarded the title of Hero of Uzbekistan.

Abdulla Oripov wrote his first poem "Bird" when he studied at the university. Abdulla Oripov's "Spring", "My first love", "Autumn", "Cancer", "Uzbekistan", "Listening to the prayer", "Othello", "Mirage", "To the sea", "Malamat stones", "Golden fish" ", "Yuzma-yuz", "Genetika" and other poems are a bright example of Uzbek literature of the second half of the 20th century.

In 1965, his first poetry collection "Mitty Star" was published. It was followed by "My eyes are on your way" (1967), "Mother" (1969), "Ruhim" (1971), "Uzbekistan", "Qasida" (1972), "Khotirot" (1974), "Yurtim". Wind" (1974), "Awe" (1979), "Fortress of Salvation" (1981), "The Dream of Years" (1984), "Bridge of Faith" (1989), "Prayer" (19992), "Haj notebook" (1995), "Sailanma" (1996) poetry collections were published.

Abdulla Oripov wrote the epics "The Way to Heaven" (1978), "The Doctor and Death" (1980), "Ranjkom", "Sahibqiron" (1996).

"Sarah's Works" by Abdulla Oripov, a four-volume collection of 2000-2001, was published.

Abdulla Oripov is the author of the National Anthem of the Republic of Uzbekistan adopted on December 10, 1992 at the eleventh session of the Supreme Council of the Republic of Uzbekistan.

The poet translated Dante Alighieri's "Divine Comedy", the works of N. Nekrasov, L. Ukrainka, T. Shevchenko, K. Kuliyev and others into Uzbek.

Abdulla Oripov dedicates his poems to his Motherland. In the poem "Autumn in Uzbekistan" he expresses the beauty of his motherland with love and sophistication:

This autumn, the ripe fruit of the gardens,
I will throw it in the ant row.
The owner of apple cider vinegar,
Old people make wrinkles.
A star shines at the pole,
The sky is also dark - its original color.
Autumn like Khizr wearing a yellow cloak,
Truly it is the season of wise souls.
Alas, my springs are gone,
Cancer remained until it was soaked in sweat.
Waiting for the end of the great show,
I wandered through the seasons.

Islam Karimov said that Abdulla Oripov's poetry is important for the current stage of development of spirituality and enlightenment.

On January 12, 2007, at the Cabinet of Ministers of the Republic of Uzbekistan, General Director of the Copyright Protection Agency of Uzbekistan Abdullah Oripov was awarded the high-level "WIPO Creativity Award" gold medal for his creative contribution to the treasury of world culture.

The memory of the poet will always live in our hearts.

Definition of Mòjaz village

Now I would like to tell you about the village where I was born. I will tell you about the history of the village of Karashokh, which I heard from the elders of our village. There are many guesses about the origin of the name of our village. He took care of him and brought him here from the people of his village. The people of the neighborhood started to live here. And the name of our village gradually began to be called Karashokh in honor of the king.

Many great people have grown up in our village. One of them is a learned dervish, popularly known as White Father and Grandfather. Archaeologists from Namangan state that this person was one of Ahmed Yassavi's students.

In our village, a mausoleum and a shrine were built in honor of this person, and pilgrims from different countries regularly visit him.

I am sure that in the future there will be people who will introduce the name of this village to the whole world. Because the generation of great people will be great.

A fairy tale for children
Young lamb

Once upon a time, once upon a time, there was a wolf and a fox, and a crow and a sparrow. In short, a flock of sheep lived on a hill. He was always walking away from his mother. Then his mother was always telling him not to do this and explaining the danger of it. But the sheep did not listen to any of them. One day, a pack of wolves approached the place where the sheep lived. Immediately, all the sheep ran to a safe place. But our little horned hero, instead of following them, went to other strange places and got lost because it was dark. Suddenly, a wild wolf appeared in front of him.The lamb was very scared and screamed with all its voice, but no one could hear it. And the wolf was preparing to eat it. It opened its mouth so much that...

Fortunately, Olapar came to save him. Seeing this, he ran away without looking back.

The little lamb arrived home safely. He returned to his mother and promised not to smile by her side.

They are unforgettable

September 2, 2013. Knowledge Day. Early morning. The school yard is crowded with people. That day I got up earlier than ever. The reason was that today was the first time I was going to school as a student. I waited a long time for the time to pass. I was ready at six o'clock. I was very excited. Finally, it was time. My best friend Kamoliddin called me to school. We went to school together. We were also happy. It was a great event. After the event, we all entered our new classroom together with our class leader Mukarramkhan Sirojiddinova. We received the president's gifts. Everyone was in a great mood. Our teacher introduced himself to us. That day was very enjoyable. I made new friends. I was a good student in all subjects, but my one fault was that I did not follow the rules of etiquette. In the middle of the 2nd grade, after the dictation, i.e. control, our teacher told me to leave the room and no longer study in this class. . That day I was very disappointed with our teacher. Now I know that everyone wanted to raise me as a real student. They wanted to help me learn all the subjects. I am very grateful to Mother Mukarramkhan Khoji. May she always be healthy.

In the future, I will definitely try to become a real person who will benefit our country and people. For this, the knowledge you gave me is a solid foundation. Thank you, teacher!

My favorite teacher

At school, everyone has a teacher whom they respect more than everyone else. I, like everyone else, have a teacher like her. This is Adibakhan Mosayeva, a hardworking and dedicated woman. This woman is the reason for my achievements in the subject of mother tongue and literature. I have learned the secrets of this subject since the 5th grade they have been teaching me. He is a real leader with the ability to teach. He is a pedagogue. I always ask him for help in any matter. .
Teacher! I am grateful for all the knowledge you have given me. May your family members, children, and the rest of us, your students, be happy. May you live long! Never get tired of spreading the light of knowledge to your students like us.
I would also like to thank my passionate teachers. I am always grateful to you:
Hazratkulova Dilfuza
Sharobiddinova Nafosat
Gulsora Saidoripovna
Ziyoda Nizomiddinova
Zubayda Ummataliyeva
Holy Nishonova
Durdona Gaynazarova

In addition, to the board of our school, which created all the conditions in the school:
Director Jamoldin Mominov
MMIBDO' to Akhliddin Azimov
I would like to express my gratitude to O'IBDO' Vahidjon Nizomiddinov

About my grandmother

Now I want to tell you the meaning of my life about my grandmother.
I grew up in my grandmother's hands since I was a child. My grandmother helped me in every way. I love my grandmother because of that. I can't imagine living without her. I come home from school or my extracurriculars and I look for my grandmother. When my grandmother goes to visit any of our relatives, I feel like something is missing.
May Allah give my grandmother a long life. May she always be a counselor by my side. If I look at the path of my grandmother's life, I will face a lot of difficulties. But my grandmother is a patient and persevering woman. She bravely overcame all of this. If God wills, I will be able to finish my studies and start working. If I find my way in life, I will definitely take my grandmother to Hajj. This is my lifelong dream.
Now I'm working on it: I'm studying, I'm searching, I'm building a foundation for my life.
My grandmother always helps me. She created the conditions for my studies. I will definitely return these favors 100 times.
Grandma, I love you. May my happiness always be safe.

Our School

Our school also has its own history. Our school was an organization before achieving this status. However, the head of the organization moved the building of his organization to another place, not letting the students, i.e. the youth of his neighborhood, travel 2 km to another school with difficulties in the mud in the winter and in the heat in the autumn. Then the students were lucky enough to go to the school of our neighborhood. My parents still bless the head of that organization. People in our neighborhood also pray for that person to be in the Gardens of Paradise. This is how our school was established. Although it has been almost fifty years, it still creates conditions for young people to get education.

But as mentioned, our school building was an organization. Therefore, the rooms are not adapted for classes. It was extremely uncomfortable for young students. There is not enough space between the board and the student's desk. This has a very negative effect on the vision of students. This situation, which can lead to bad consequences, can be eliminated only by building a new building. In our school, we have difficulty conducting laboratory classes because the chemistry, biology, and physics rooms are not fully renovated. Because it does not contain all the necessary reactants. This leads us to not fully mastering it and leaving a gap in our knowledge. We want all subjects to have their own room. We hope that the mother tongue classes will be in rooms with visual aids and this science environment. Having air conditioning in all rooms also affects the student's learning. Because due to the heat, the receptive part of the students' brain stops working. As a result, the student does not understand the lesson. A student who does not understand one or two lessons will lose interest in the lesson. In the end, the society accepts another useless person.

That is why, if the schools meet all the requirements set by the state, if sufficient conditions are created for the students and teachers, the students would be eager to learn, and the teacher would be in a hurry to spread the knowledge.

This is my dream school

Humanity

Humanity is making a lot of changes in the world. Day by day, news, updates in every field continue at a rapid pace. Especially great changes are taking place in electric power, robotics, and education. Thirty years ago, our people used a candle, but today they use an electric lamp. Twenty-thirty years ago, did our people have concepts about robots? No, of course. But now almost all factories are using robots. We all had no idea about messengers such as Instagram, Telegram, and Facebook, which have become our daily needs. These have become popular in the last five years. Newly constructed buildings and structures are also among them. In any case, these news should serve good. We don't need news that opens new wars, after all. We can create news like this. For this, we need to read a lot of books, seek new knowledge and achieve new successes.

The Republic of Uzbekistan is being renewed day by day. Not only our country, but also laws and decisions are changing. Not only the decisions, but also the amendments being made to the Constitution of the Republic of Uzbekistan, which is the main law of our country.

All this is for Uzbekistan, which is being updated! I think that by 2050, Uzbekistan will be radically changed and renewed. In particular, getting electricity from the Sun will increase. Today's young people become knowledgeable, intelligent, in a word, ideal people. New, beautiful, attractive schools are being built. But among the observed changes there may be negative ones. In 2050, there may be a water shortage in Uzbekistan. The island may completely dry up and become a desert zone. It's up to you and me to prevent this. It is necessary to use water carefully, use it only when necessary, do not throw away water (drinking water) without closing the tap. Only then the above cases will not be observed. We are all responsible for this, dear ones. Most of the animals included in the "Red Book" are exterminated by members of illegal hunting. We all have to fight against it. If we continue to think about news and changes, there will be big changes in banking and finance. Inflation, which is the most painful point of the state and people, can also be observed. This is not a secret to any of us.

During our speech, we thought about the modernizing Uzbekistan and its future. Summarizing these thoughts, we can say that New Uzbekistan is yours, New Uzbekistan is ours, and New Uzbekistan belongs to all of us. It is necessary for all of us to act as one in order for the renewal of time to be in our favor. Let's conclude with the poem "The Future" by Ozodbek Yigitaliyev:

The future is ours
Time is ours
Updating
Life is ours!

This book is a collection of *Ozodbek Yigitaliyev*'s original works. Despite his young age, He is one of the ambitious and hardworking young people. His entry into literature comes with this book. This collection contains Ozodbek's memoirs dedicated to the memory of outstanding representatives of our literature, global and popular topics of the time, his feelings and experiences, as well as his first poetic works.

www.ingramcontent.com/pod-product-compliance
Lightning Source LLC
LaVergne TN
LVHW010424070526
838199LV00064B/5420